Public Library District of Columbia

EARTH'S CONTINENTS

Asia

by Mary Lindeen

Asia is the largest **continent** in the world. One-third of all the land on Earth is in Asia.

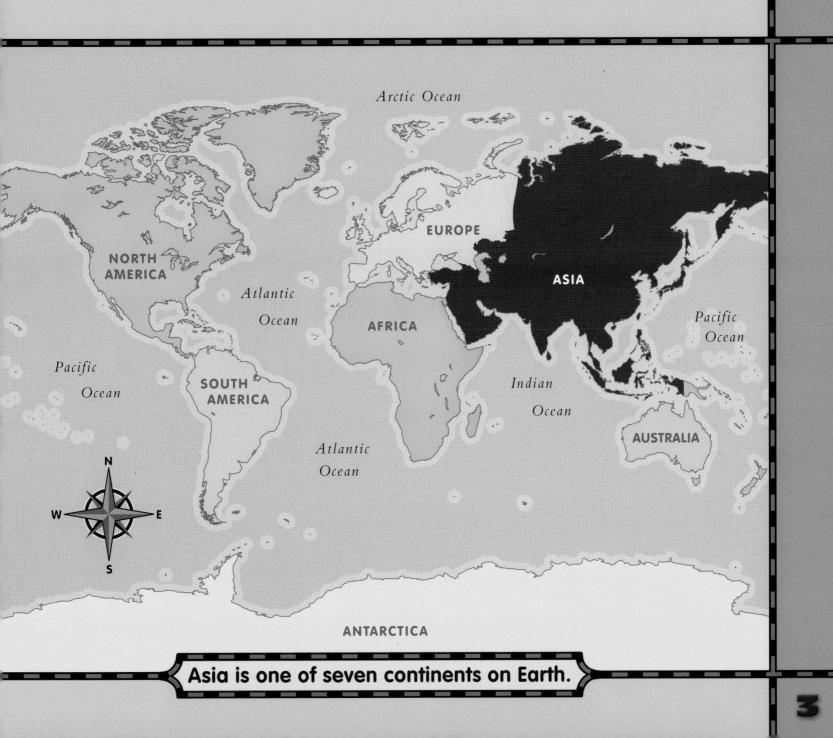

Arctic Ocean

EUROPE

ASIA

NORTH
AMERICA

Atlantic
Ocean

AFRICA

Pacific
Ocean

Pacific
Ocean

SOUTH
AMERICA

Indian
Ocean

Atlantic
Ocean

AUSTRALIA

N
W   E
S

ANTARCTICA

Asia is one of seven continents on Earth.

Many **islands** in the Pacific Ocean are part of Asia. Volcanoes made these islands.

Indonesia, an Asian **country**, is made up of more than 17,500 islands.

The highest mountain in the world is in Asia. It is called Mount Everest. Asia also has flat **grasslands**.

Mount Everest is 29,035 feet (8,850 meters) tall.

There are deserts in some parts of Asia. In other places, there are farms and flowing rivers.

The Mekong River is in Asia.

Most of the rice grown in the world comes from Asia. Tea and fruit are some of Asia's other crops.

Fruits and vegetables are sold at some Asian markets.

Asia has many countries. The country of China has more people than any other country in the world. Other parts of Asia have hardly any people.

Beijing is a busy city in China. Many people live and work there.

Asia is home to many kinds of people. They enjoy different special events. Many people **celebrate** the start of a new year.

This woman is dressed up for a New Year's parade.

Asia has many buildings that are thousands of years old. It also has cities that are growing.

The Golden Temple in Japan is very old.

Asia has so many different things to see and do. Where would you like to go first?

Many people visit the Taj Mahal in India, an Asian country.

Glossary

celebrate (SEL-uh-brayt): People celebrate when they do something fun for a special event. Some people in Asia celebrate the start of a new year.

continent (KON-tuh-nent): A continent is one of seven large land areas on Earth. Asia is a continent.

country (KUN-tree): A country is an area of land with its own government. China is a country in Asia.

grasslands (GRASS-lands): Grasslands are large open areas of grass where animals can graze. Some parts of Asia have grasslands.

islands (EYE-lands): Islands are areas of land surrounded by water. The continent of Asia includes many islands.

parade (puh-RAYD): People marching for a holiday is called a parade. In some Asian countries, people celebrate the new year with a parade.

To Find Out More

Books

Fowler, Allan. *Asia*. Danbury, CT: Children's Press, 2002.

Kalman, Bobbie, and Rebecca Sjonger. *Explore Asia*. New York: Crabtree Publishing, 2009.

Sayre, April Pulley. *Greetings, Asia!* Brookfield, CT: Millbrook Press, 2003.

Web Sites

Visit our Web site for links about Asia: *childsworld.com/links*

Note to Parents, Teachers, and Librarians: We routinely verify our Web links to make sure they are safe and active sites. So encourage your readers to check them out!

Index

About the Author

Mary Lindeen is an elementary school teacher who turned her love of children and books into a career in publishing. She has written and edited many library books and literacy programs. She also enjoys traveling with her son, Benjamin, whenever and wherever she can.

On the cover: The Great Wall of China is thousands of years old.

Published by The Child's World®
1980 Lookout Drive • Mankato, MN 56003-1705
800-599-READ • www.childsworld.com

ACKNOWLEDGMENTS
The Child's World®: Mary Berendes, Publishing Director
The Design Lab: Design, page, and map production
Red Line Editorial: Editorial direction

PHOTO CREDITS: CPW/iStockphoto, cover; Rob Broek/iStockphoto, 5; Big Stock Photo, 7, 9, 11, 17, 19; Yong Hian Lim/iStockphoto, 13; John Leung/Shutterstock, 15; Erick Nguyen/iStockphoto, 21

Printed in the United States of America in Mankato, Minnesota.
November 2009
F11460

LIBRARY OF CONGRESS CATALOGING-IN-PUBLICATION DATA
Lindeen, Mary.
  Asia / by Mary Lindeen.
    p. cm. — (Earth's continents)
  Includes index.
  ISBN 978-1-60253-348-6 (library bound : alk. paper)
  1. Asia—Juvenile literature. I. Title. II. Series.
  DS5.L56 2010
  915—dc22
                                    2009030009